Black Propaganda
by John Pether

Report No.12, December 1998
© John Pether and Bletchley Park Trust 1998

Contents

1.	Introduction	3
2.	The move to Woburn	4
3.	Black printed material	4
4.	The first Black Radio stations	6
5.	Denis Sefton Delmer	8
6.	Delmer's first research unit	9
7.	Aspidistra	12
8.	Big Bertha	15
9.	The final period	16
10.	Bibliography	18

Appendix: Research Units (radio transmissions)   19 - 26

BLACK PROPAGANDA

1. INTRODUCTION
Throughout the Second World War, in many houses in villages near here, another kind of war was being wrought against the Axis powers in Europe. Some may even say sinister; this was the Black Propaganda war. Propaganda can be divided into either black or white with various shades of grey between. White propaganda does not conceal or attempt to conceal its point of origin, indeed the white operations were carried out during the war by:-

a. The broadcasts by the BBC to Germany and enemy occupied countries.
b. The many leaflets dropped on the enemy by the RAF, bearing the stamp of the British government.

Black propaganda, however, is designed to give the impression that it originates from within the country it is aimed at, whilst grey does not give any clear indication of its origin.

There are various methods of conducting black propaganda, through the written or the spoken word or the combination of both. These methods can be summarised as follows:

1. Black radio stations.
2. Black printed matter.
3. Agents.

Black radio stations can be operated in three distinct ways:

1. The station can be made to appear to be operated inside the country it is addressing, either as an outright opposition group or as a pseudo-patriotic group subtly exposing corruption in high places.
2. The station can be used to convey news and information to agents operating inside an enemy country for use in the production of black material.
3. The station can be used to counterfeit the official broadcasts within the country concerned.

Indeed, by the end of the war, there had been some 48 Black stations, initially known as Freedom Stations but later they were called Research Units or RU's, broadcasting to enemy and occupied countries. Some of these stations were short-lived while others operated for several years.

The stations ranged from German left wing to German religious, to those aimed at the occupied countries to assist in creating resistance to the occupying forces. The output of some was designed to undermine the quisling governments that were set up in occupied countries. The total combined output of these stations was well over 10,000 programmes.

Black printed material can be written in a form so that it appears to come from opposition groups working within the enemy country, with the aim of undermining the morale of the fighting forces and civilian population. It can also be in the form of government departmental instructions designed to create confusion within the administrative machine. It can also be in the form of forged clothing and food coupons etc. aimed at undermining the economy and official rationing systems. Many printed items supported material being broadcast by the RU's.

The output of black printed material was large, with print runs ranging from a few to several million at a time.

2. THE MOVE TO WOBURN
Both black and white propaganda production were controlled by a secret department, eventually known as the Political Warfare Executive (PWE). The formation of the PWE was rather convoluted but basically it was descended from two other secret organisations:- Dept. Electra House (EH) of the Foreign Office and SO1 of SOE. Almost immediately Germany surrendered the PWE ceased to exist.

Dept. EH was mobilised at the end of August 1939 when the outbreak of war seemed imminent, and because it was assumed that London would be bombed immediately, steps were taken to evacuate most of the staff out of London.

Initial arrangements were made by one of its staff, Leo Russell, a relation of the Duke of Bedford, for Dept EH to take over the stable wing and riding school on the Duke's estate at Woburn in Bedfordshire.

When Germany invaded Poland on September 1st 1939, Dept EH evacuated to their country headquarters at Woburn. As only a few staff knew the existence of the country headquarters (CHQ), members were told to make their way to the Sugar Loaf Hotel, located on the Watling Street in Dunstable, where upon arrival they were told to ask for a Mr. Gibbs-Smith (Admin Officer CHQ). Once the new arrivals' identity had been established, Mr. Gibbs-Smith would either supply a sketch map shewing directions to Woburn or arrange transport. Over the next few days some 60 staff were to settle in at Woburn to start work on the propaganda war.

3. BLACK PRINTED MATERIAL
The fakes and forgery unit of the PWE did not become really active until the spring of 1942. However, ideas in the production of printed material were first instigated at the time of the Munich crisis of 1938, by the then Section D of SIS. Dept EH's printing side did not emerge until the autumn of 1940, rather amateurishly and without inheriting anything really useful from Section D. At that time Dept EH's main task was the production of white leaflets for the RAF to drop over Germany.

Early black initiatives included:
1. A rumour of the ill effects of a high starch diet.
2. An attempt to undermine the credit of the German bank Zeiler & Co. by a letter campaign.
3. The production of fake destination labels used to route railway goods wagons around the continent. These were planted by willing helpers to divert consignments intended for Germany to other destinations.
4. It was also suggested that some sort of apparatus could be constructed to project propaganda images in the sky above the German lines.

In November 1941 Ellic Howe joined the newly-formed PWE. He was a printer by trade and was very interested in the history of printing, European in particular. Before the war, on his travels in Europe, he would collect specimens of jobbing printing, for example commercial stationery, letter heads, hotel bills, leaflets etc. From this he was able to identify nearly all the current type faces or fonts in current use on the continent. It also demonstrated to him how compositors would lay out the text, and which fonts were used for particular jobs.

At the beginning of the war Howe was a Lance Corporal in the 27th Searchlight Regiment, Royal Engineers. He became a Sergeant Major at the Headquarters Anti-Aircraft Command, Stanmore. Here he was put in charge of the Registry which was a distribution centre for secret documents and it was from here he found his way into the PWE. Howe and his miniscule unit, with an eventual staff of 3, found themselves in an office in a remote corner on the 6th floor of Bush House.

Although the PWE and its predecessors were using several jobbing printing companies for their black printing production, they were having difficulties locating and obtaining the correct materials at short notice. Howe's connexions within the print trade enabled him to locate quickly German Gothic type face, papers and inks for the production of forged material.

SOE agents working on the continent obtained many original items which were smuggled back to this country. This enabled paper manufacturers to produce identical papers with the correct watermarks where necessary. In one instance when it was required to fake the letterhead of the Reichsbank, difficulties were encountered in obtaining a suitable match for the paper until it was discovered that the paper used for the bottle labels of a well known brand of beer provided a near identical match.

Maryland, the Duchess of Bedford's Cottage Hospital in Woburn, already taken over by the PWE predecessors, became home to Harold Keeble's print shop. Although chiefly concerned in the production of white leaflets it did help in the production of a considerable amount of black material.

The Home Counties Newspaper Group with its presses based at Luton and Leagrave printed numerous items, in particular the daily newspaper Nachrichten für der Truppe, which was dropped in millions over German soldiers in Western Europe in the last year of the war. Although described as dirty off-white rather than black, every night for nearly a year this paper was published. The Special Leaflet Squadron of the USAF dropped the specially designed leaflet bombs which could hold 80,000 copies. The bombs were made of waxed paper 60in. long by 18in. diameter. A cordite fuse split the bomb at an altitude of 1000 feet, distributing its payload over about a square mile.

Two other items of particular interest which the Home Counties Newspaper Group printed for the PWE were when Hess unexpectedly parachuted into Scotland.

One consisted of two fake pages from the Volkischer Beobachter, the official Nazi newspaper. The pages are identical to the genuine paper apart from a small article inserted in the bottom right-hand corner of one page. It reads:

Stories in the foreign press to the effect that Hess's wife and 4 year old son are in the custody of the Gestapo are the malicious inventions of enemy propaganda. At the present time Frau Hess and her son are in a mental hospital in Thuringia.

The second was a copy of the Daily Telegraph dated 20th June 1941. Only three copies were produced and were identical to the original apart from an article which gives an account of an interview between the former US Ambassador of Belgium and Hitler. In the fake copy a passage was changed, to the effect that Hess was suffering from an incurable mental disease and that his son had inherited it.

The plan was that the Volkischer Beobachter would be given to Hess followed by the Daily Telegraph, in the hope that he would read both articles and break his silence. Whether or not he read them, the plan backfired as neither had the desired effect.

There were numerous letter campaigns carried out with letters being posted in neutral and occupied countries, the Poles being the most successful at posting material within Germany. They didn't even have to buy the stamps, as they were being supplied with forgeries printed in this country by Waterlow and Sons, the security printers.

4. THE FIRST BLACK RADIO STATIONS

A certain Dr Carl Spieker who had been a member of the German Civil Service in the early 1930's, had fallen foul of the Nazi regime and was obliged to emigrate to France in 1933, where he became a prominent member of the German Freedom Party. This had been formed by German Social Democratic refugees and concerned mainly with the smuggling of leaflets into Germany before the frontiers closed.

From the Autumn of 1939 Dr. Spieker and his associates ran a short wave radio station purporting to be broadcasting within Germany but which was in fact located just outside Paris. Deutsche Freiheitssender, as it was known, was forced to close down with the approach of the German Army.

EH was aware of Spieker's activities and with the help of the Deuxième Bureau (the French equivalent of MI5), arrangements were made to bring him back to England under the respectable name of Mr. Turner. With his experience he would be ideal to start black broadcasts to Germany from the safety of this country.

Dr Spieker's Das Wahre Deutschland (The True Germany) went on the air on the 26th May 1940. Later that year several other Freedom Stations, as they were initially known, started broadcasting to enemy and occupied countries. Later these freedom stations became known as research units or RU's.

G2 Sender der Europäischen Revolution was the next to go on the air, on 7th October 1940, it was a left wing station, with its production team headed by Richard Crossman billeted at Dawn Edge (DE), Aspley Guise. This station was followed a month later by two French stations, F1, Radio Inconnue and F2, Radio Travail, both subversive in their content, both using obscene language to denounce the Germans. The small production teams for these stations were accommodated at the Old Rectory at Toddington (TOR), a village a few miles south of Woburn.

W1, Radio Italia went on the air around this time, spreading detrimental stories about the Germans and encouraging listeners to hoard items that were in short supply.

The programmes were initially recorded at Whaddon Hall, a large country house three miles north-west from Bletchley, where a recording studio had been established, but as the department expanded another large house, Wavendon Tower, was taken over and recording studios were established there, becoming known as Simpsons, the name Simpson merely being taken from name of the nearby village a few miles north-west of Woburn.

A transmitter site was established at Gawcott, two miles south-west of Buckingham. Here two 7.5kw short wave transmitters were installed. These two transmitters were given the names Geranium and Gardenia. However, it was soon realised that additional facilities would be required, so an identical setup was established at Potsgrove just south of Woburn Abbey. The transmitters there were named Poppy and Pansy.

The programmes were recorded onto 16in diameter glass based discs at a speed of 33 r.p.m. which limited the length of each programme to a maximum of 20 minutes. Initially these were recorded at Whaddon and played over GPO private wires to the Gawcott transmitter. However, when Simpsons was established, because of the security risk the discs were usually taken by road to the transmitter sites and played there.

The production teams for these research units were billeted in requisitioned houses in surrounding villages. Each house was managed by a resident officer whose wife normally acted as housekeeper.

As many of the staff of the RU's were made up of foreign nationals, including German and Italian POW's, security had to be tight and efforts were made to isolate them from the local people. They were not allowed to make telephone calls, any letters they needed to post were sent to London for posting and any incoming mail for them was sent to a P.O. Box in London.

For the first 14 months of the war, Dept EH continued with its work at Woburn but towards the end of 1941 large-scale developments were to take place with the formation of the Political Warfare Executive and the arrival of Denis Sefton Delmer. It was decided that the newly formed PWE headquarters should be back in London on the three upper floors of Bush House. Consequently, early in 1942 the majority of the staff vacated Woburn and were relocated back in London, whilst the staff engaged in black propaganda and white leaflet production would remain. The PWE still retained possession of the Riding School which provided office accommodation for the staff administering the 16 or so Research Units, as the black radio stations were now known, that had been established by this time. The production teams for these had by now taken over some 12 private houses in the Woburn area. The activities of these RU's were totally outside the control of the BBC and were classified 'Most Secret'.

5. DENIS SEFTON DELMER
Born in Berlin to Australian parents, he spent his childhood there. The family was repatriated to England in 1917, where he eventually won a scholarship to Lincoln College, Oxford. After graduating, he took up a career in journalism and in 1928 became the Berlin correspondent for the Daily Express. It was this position that enabled him to become acquainted with Hitler, Göring, Himmler and many other Nazi personalities. When the war broke out he made his way back to England; being bilingual in English and German, he thought he would be useful in one of the intelligence services. However; with his background the security services initially viewed him with suspicion.

His first job was a part time position with the BBC that entailed improving the BBC's German service, a job that earned him a position in the Sonderfahndungsliste. This was a list of Britons who were to be arrested and handed over to the Gestapo, if the Germans had successfully invaded Britain.

In November 1940 SIS (MI6) asked Delmer to do some work for them in Lisbon using his employment with the Daily Express as a cover. In Lisbon he met many German refugees who updated him on what life was like in war time Germany. These people also gave useful information about important electronics firms such as Askania and Lorenz. Early in 1941 Delmer received a telegram from Leonard Ingrams, Under Secretary at the Ministry of Economic Warfare and liaison officer to the PWE, telling him to return to England, where an important job awaited him. Back in England he was taken to Woburn where he signed the Official Secrets Act; he was then installed in an office in a building in Berkeley Square back in London. It would be a couple of months before he was asked to create a new right wing research unit, the main reason for his recruitment. Ingrams asked Delmer to outline a plan for this new RU with no holds barred.

6. DELMER'S FIRST RESEARCH UNIT

Analysing the contents within the existing BBC and RU broadcasts to Germany, Delmer realised that they were being aimed at the wrong people - those who were already against Hitler and the Nazi regime. Delmer's plan for the RU was to aim at the unconverted, by undermining Hitler, not by opposing him, but by pretending to be all for him and his war. The plan was put forward to Ingrams, Crossman and Rex Leeper, Delmer's departmental chiefs who minuted it a novel and promising idea. Please go ahead with all speed.

The plan proposed that it would be a shortwave radio station, initially aimed at the knob twiddling radio operators within the German military services, itself purporting to be some sort of German military station. In between the pseudo-cipher messages the operator would broadcast outspoken views on what was going on within the Nazi regime. These views while being spiced up with plenty of inside information and scandal would show him to be loyal to the Führer, but expose a growing split between the conservative officers of the army and the radical members of the Nazi Party.

Delmer decided that the operator of the station would call himself 'Der Chef'. Der Chef was the title that Delmer had heard party officials refer to Hitler, whilst he had accompanied them on campaigns during 1932 and 1933.

The station, G3, was given the callsign Gustav Siegfried Eins:- signallers' German for George Sugar One:- GS1. Delmer left it to the listeners to decide what it stood for - Geheimsender 1 - Generalstab 1, or Gurkensalat 1 - Cucumber Salad as Ingrams suggested.

Delmer moved into Larchfield (LF), a house in Aspley Guise, not far from Woburn and set up his production team for his new RU there. His wife Isabel acted as housekeeper and his production team initially consisted of Johannes Reinholz, a scriptwriter and journalist who had escaped out of Germany in 1939, Max Braun another refugee from Germany who was an anti-Nazi Socialist, and Paul Sanders whose real name was Peter Seckelmann, an author of detective stories who had moved to England from Berlin in 1938. Here he became a corporal in the Pioneer Corps and had volunteered for special duties, and as a result had been passed on to Delmer. Because of his clipped metallic accent it was he whom Delmer chose to be Der Chef.

On May 23rd 1941 Delmer and Paul Sanders arrived at Simpsons and recorded the first broadcast for GS1. The discs were then taken by road to the transmitter sites for broadcasting. The initial programme lasted about ten minutes and was broadcast on two frequencies hourly at seven minutes to the hour. A similar procedure was followed every day for nearly 2½ years.

The first few broadcasts were perhaps rather amateurish but as the production team gained confidence, later productions soon became more professional.

It was suggested to Delmer that the station should have a signature tune at the beginning of each transmission, just to make it easier for the listeners to identify it. The German equivalent to the BBC, the Deutschlandsender, used the opening bars of an 18th century folksong played on a carillon.

> *Ub immer treu und Redlichkeit*
> Always practice truth and probity...

... tinkled the Deutschlandsender and now Gustav Siegfried Eins burst out into the ether with the second line to the song on what sounded like a worn out barrack room piano:-

> *Bis an dein Kuhles Grab*
> Until your cool cool grave

The initial broadcast followed the format:

> *Here is Gustav Siegfried Eins... Here is Gustav Siegfried Eins,*

which Der Chef repeated for about 45 seconds. And then

> *calling Gustav Siegfried 18.... calling Gustav Siegfried 18, Message from Gustav Siegfried Eins.*

There then followed a low grade cipher message, which could easily be broken by the Reich Central Security Office. The message gave details of a secret meeting to be held at a Union Cinema, and as there were hundreds of Union cinemas all over Germany, Delmer envisaged numerous leather-coated Gestapo Officers wasting their time searching these cinemas for this non- existent meeting. With their radio direction finding equipment they would soon realise the transmission was coming from England and believe the message was for a meeting of British Agents.

Der Chef then started answering queries that had resulted from previous transmissions, which was done to give the impression that this was not the first broadcast, again to cause confusion to the German Security Monitors.

The first broadcast coincided with the arrival of Hess in this country and in the transmission Der Chef included a list of suspected associates who had been arrested. The names were real but the list was fictitious. Delmer was delighted a few days later when German newspapers reported that some of the people on the list had been arrested and interrogated by the Gestapo.

Der Chef ended the broadcast with,

> *I shall repeat this broadcast, all being well, every hour at seven minutes to the hour.*

Delmer believed that this would give the impression to the listeners that Der Chef was being pursued by the Gestapo.

In the following broadcasts Der Chef would attack local Nazi party officials. exposing black market activities, racketeering, sex scandals and other illicit activities.

The information used by Der Chef came from a number of sources - lists of names compiled from German newspapers; POWs were secretly recorded whilst in their cells which gave Delmer the latest barrack room slang and gossip; numerous letters, intercepted on their way to German nationals in the neutral USA, were opened and read by censors. All this information was stored in an ever increasing card index file for future use.

With the increasing audience of Gustav Siegfried Eins on the continent, despite the jamming, more evidence of reception, known as 'come backs', started to filter back to Delmer. It even fooled the Americans. How could a radio station that often referred to Churchill as a "flat-footed bastard of a drunken Jew" and the King as "stuttering fool" originate from Britain? In September 1941 the American Embassy in Berlin reported to Washington the existence of an illegal broadcasting station called Gustav Siegfried Eins supposedly transmitting inside Germany, operating daily on the 31.5 metre band at seven minutes to the hour....

...using violent and unbelievably obscene language, it criticises the actions of the Nazi Party especially members of the SS. A very large number of Germans listen to this station.

GS1 even had its admirers in Goebbels' Propaganda Ministry and a report from the SOE had it that a German working for the Propaganda Ministry, having a drink in a bar in neutral Stockholm, got bragging to an obvious Englishman and was heard to say

' ...even the anti-Nazi propaganda is done better by the Germans themselves than by the British. I tell you just outside Berlin there is a man with a wireless station, who calls himself Der Chef - everybody listens to him. He has the support of high army officers and he reveals scandals about the party which are most effective. Listen, I'll tell you some good advice. The British Secret Service ought to contact Der Chef and see if they could not come to an understanding with him.'

Der Chef continued with his broadcasts until 18th November 1943. Greater plans were inhand and it was decided for Der Chef to disappear. The answer was simple - the Gestapo had tracked him down at long last. Listeners in Germany heard the burst of machine gun fire amongst cries of 'got you, you swinehound!'

Unfortunately the engineers at the Potsgrove transmitter, not speaking German, failed to realise the significance of the last recording and so Der Chef died again an hour later when, as usual the recording was re-broadcast. Whether any listeners noticed we shall probably never know.

7. ASPIDISTRA

Early in 1940 the technical feasibility of breaking into the Volksempfanger was discussed, the object being to reach into German homes, in which at that time over 3 million of these domestic radio receivers had been installed with the aid of Government subsidies. The idea was that the Goebbels propaganda mouthpiece, the Reichsprogramme which was relayed from Berlin to transmitters in 12 key cities around Germany, could be received by the working classes. These receivers were said to have been deliberately designed to be deaf in an effort to prevent German civilians from listening to foreign stations, but this was probably due to the need to produce a cheap receiver rather than to Nazi policy. However, a powerful medium wave transmitter would be required to do this.

In the spring of 1941, under the guidance of Hugh Dalton (Ministry of Economic Warfare), Anthony Eden (Foreign Office) and Brenden Bracken (Ministry of Information), the then SO1 developed a plan to broadcast on German wavelengths. The plan was shown to Churchill for his approval; his reply was simply 'Pray proceed'. For this plan Delmer would be asked to create two new black stations, firstly Deutsche Kurzwellensender Atlantik - the German Shortwave Radio Atlantic. Mainly aimed at the crews of U boats, the German listeners would soon shorten it to Atlantik-sender. And later Soldatensender Calais aimed at the Army and Luftwaffe.

The plan also involved the purchase of a 500kw medium-wave transmitter from RCA in America. This had originally been built for station WJZ in New Jersey but it far exceeded the 50kw maximum allowed for commercial stations and the authorities would not license it.

Richard Gambier-Parry, head of technical control for the newly formed PWE submitted a purchase proposal on behalf of the British government. It cost an estimated £165,000. It was to be by far the most powerful medium wave transmitter in Europe and was given the code name Aspidistra.

Gambier-Parry sent Harold Robin, who was directly under him, to the RCA factory in America, where he spent the summer of 1941 familiarising himself with the equipment. He also supervised the modifications that increased its power to 600kw.

However, back in England there were to be problems in finding a site for Aspidistra and the BBC were objecting to the PWE's plans. The BBC were worried that the new radio stations would start an all out war of the airwaves and the Germans would start jamming the BBC home service transmissions which up until now had not happened and also the BBC would be singled out as a target for German bombers. After much heated discussion it was pointed out that intelligence sources indicated that the enemy had no transmitter of the power required, nor the resources to undertake to construct one to carry out any effective jamming of the BBC. It was also agreed that the BBC could use the new transmitter to supplement its overseas broadcasts when it wasn't being used by the PWE.

The site for Aspidistra was originally to be a disused gravel quarry near Woburn. A large purpose built studio complex was established in a quiet corner of the Woburn Abbey estate at Milton Bryan. However, Robin insisted that the site for the transmitter should be much further south to be nearer to the Continent. Several sites were chosen but each time objections were raised by either the Air Ministry or the BBC. In desperation a meeting was held at Whitehall with representatives from the Air Ministry, the Post Office, BBC, Home Office and any other interested parties. Eventually a site was found at King's Standing, near Crowborough, 620 feet above sea level.

Around 70 acres of land were fenced off and as Aspidistra was to be built underground a 50 feet deep hole was excavated This was done by a Canadian Army road-building unit that was stationed nearby who gladly took up the challenge. According to Robin they seemed to survive the six weeks it took them to excavate the hole on a diet solely of beer. The building was then built in the bottom of the hole, being heavily reinforced taking the 600 strong civilian work force, working 24 hours a day, a further nine months to complete.

The equipment for Aspidistra along with the three 300 foot high masts were shipped in several consignments aboard Royal Navy ships. One consignment was lost when the convoy was attacked and the ship torpedoed.

Aspidistra was three times more powerful than any existing German medium-wave transmitters. It was also unique in that it could be changed to another frequency within the medium-wave band very quickly. In fact it could be moved to any one of six pre-selected frequencies within about five minutes. All six pre-selected frequencies could be changed to another six within two hours.

A further two 100kw shortwave transmitters were also installed at Crowborough, along with a mobile transmitter on the south coast near Dover, just to confuse the direction-finders.

Churchill had taken a great deal of interest in the project since he had given the go-ahead, and was getting impatient at the time it was taking to get Aspidistra on the air and requested a report on progress every three days.

The studio complex at Milton Bryan was built by the Ministry of Works using direct labour. The main studio block was a two-storey brick building. Again Robin's staff installed all the wiring and equipment. The GPO installed a small switchboard and provided numerous high-grade private wires to Potsgrove, Gawcott and Aspidistra at Crowborough, along with further private wires to Reuters, the Press Association and the POW interrogation centres at Latimer and Wilton Park.

Delmer's programme production team had to be increased quite dramatically to write scripts for the new stations and expanded into the Rookery at Aspley Guise, which already housed staff of another German RU. Again, great efforts were made to prevent members of different RUs from meeting at Milton Bryan. Coaches were used to bring them to and from their billets in Aspley Guise. A hostel had also been built within the complex for sleeping accommodation if required. The five-acre site was surrounded by a twelve foot high barbed wire fence and patrolled by armed Special Constables with two Alsatian dogs.

Aspidistra was ready to operate on full power on the 15th October 1942 although there were no spare valves available in the event of a failure. As a result Churchill was asked to urge President Roosevelt to speed up the manufacture of the valves by RCA.

Aspidistra was first used on 8th November 1942 to broadcast pre-recorded speeches of President Roosevelt and General Eisenhower, when it was known that the American landings in North Africa were proceeding successfully. Apart from a short-lived Italian RU, the Medium Wave Aspidistra transmitter remained in use by the BBC, to reinforce its European services, until it was required again by the PWE later the following year.

Atlantik Sender went on the air live on the 22nd March 1943 with a shrieking pipe melody as its signature tune, initially using the Potsgrove shortwave transmitter. Aimed chiefly at the Kriegsmarine U Boat crews, it was unlike Gustav Seigfried Eins; it did not use obscene and violent language, in fact it was made out to be a true forces station designed to entertain the troops, playing popular music and news stories with items subtly inserted to undermine the morale of the U boat crews. As with Gustav Seigfried Eins, the first broadcast contained items that gave the impression to the listener it had been on the air for some time. It played American jazz with a German flavour, records of the latest German hits were specially flown in by Mosquito from Stockholm. Further records were made at MB by the German equivalent of an ENSA band, which had been captured by the Eighth Army in North Africa. Marlene Dietrich was duped into making recordings in German in the belief they were for use on a German broadcast of the Voice of America.

The information that was used to write the scripts for the broadcasts came from numerous sources, but chiefly from the ever increasing number of prisoners of war being interrogated. Admiral Godfrey's Naval Intelligence Dept. NID 17z had been created to provide information. Delmer was also lucky in that he had installed at MB a Deutsche Nachrichtenburo, the German news agency DNB for short, Hellschreiber machine. This had been inadvertently left at the DNB offices in London when the war broke out and the staff fled back to Germany. A sort of cross between a radio operated teleprinter and a fascimile machine, this provided Delmer with the latest news from Goebbels' propaganda machine as it was released. In fact Atlantik Sender could broadcast the latest German sports news and the names of servicemen to receive decorations before the genuine German Forces Radio. To give Atlantik Sender further authenticity, live broadcasts of speeches given by Goebbels and Hitler over the German radio network were picked up off air at Milton Bryan and relayed over the Atlantik Sender live.

Delmer was amazed at the large number of Germans that believed Atlantik Sender was a genuine German Forces Radio; amongst the growing number of 'come backs' was a report from a POW that, for several days Atlantik Sender had been piped round the recreational huts of a German equivalent to a NAAFI by the sergeant, because he thought the music was so marvellous. Only when he was reprimanded by an Officer did he realise he had been entertaining the troops with an enemy station.

In the bulletins between the music would be subtle reports of increasing crime waves, unsolved murders, Party Officials being allowed to move away from bomber targets, people smuggling money into safe accounts in Switzerland and South America. When Delmer and his team learned that people were being evacuated during allied bombing raids on German cities, to Poland, Slovakia and other eastern areas, Atlantik Sender reported that there were epidemics of typhoid and cholera raging in the areas. All these stories along with many others were designed to make the listeners within the Kriegsmarine worry about what was happening to their families back home.

For some nine months Atlantik Sender broadcast on the shortwave bands until it was linked to the other station Soldatensender Calais. This was again made to give the impression to the listener that it was a forces station. Using the powerful Aspidistra transmitter on the medium wave band, it was aimed primarily at the German army and Luftwaffe. The idea behind this was to attract an audience among the German armed forces in the months running up to Operation Overlord. Soldatensender went on the air on 14th November 1943 and both stations carried on broadcasting until 30th April 1945, by which time they were between them on the air virtually 24 hours a day.

At the end of 1943 Aspidistra was also being used to interfere with the German ground controls transmissions to the Luftwaffe's nightfighters when the RAF was on bombing missions over Germany. The trick employed to confuse the German pilots was to record the ground control instructions on one evening and then re-transmit them the next. Aspidistra was far more powerful than the medium-wave transmitter that was used by the ground control and easily blotted it out, thus sending the nightfighters off in the wrong directions. This was known as Operation Dartboard.

8. BIG BERTHA
It came to Delmer's attention that whenever a RAF bombing raid was within around 50 miles of its target city, the local medium wave Deutschlandsender transmitter went off the air so it could not be used as a navigation aid by the RAF. Here was to be the ultimate hoax, called Big Bertha: using the powerful Aspidistra transmitter there was now a way to break into the domestic Volksempfanger, to send misleading instructions to the German civilian population.

The city of Cologne was selected to be the first target for Big Bertha. It involved training two people at Milton Bryan to imitate the local announcers used at the Cologne relay station. The RAF targeted Cologne on March 24th 1945, and informed Delmer that the transmitter would go off the air at 9.15pm. That evening the Reichsprogramme was being picked up off the air at Milton Bryan on two different frequencies, one being the Cologne frequency. The Aspidistra transmitter had been previously tuned to the

Cologne transmitter frequency but was not radiating. At around 9.15pm as expected Cologne went off the air with the approaching RAF bombers; this automatically switched on the Aspidistra transmitter, which carried on broadcasting the Reichsprogramme being picked up off the air at MB from a different relay station. The actual break in transmission was around 6 milli-seconds, hardly noticeable by the listeners in Cologne. For a short period Aspidistra carried on relaying the genuine Reichsprogramme, until a convenient point where it was faded out and the announcers at the Milton Bryan studios took over, giving out misleading information telling people to leave their homes immediately taking only essential possessions. The men were told to report for duty in readiness to defend their city against the approaching allied forces. Women and children were told to walk to specified evacuation centres, where local Nazi party officials would marshal the evacuees. In reports captured at the end of the war the hoax had been completely successful, creating confusion and panic amongst the population during the air raid.

With the co-operation of the RAF, Leipzig and Frankfurt were the next cities to be targeted using the same procedure. In the last months of the war Aspidistra was used on ten occasions for the Big Bertha hoax.

9. THE FINAL PERIOD

By the Spring of 1945, the psychological Warfare Division of SHEAF decided that after 15 May the Black and Grey Propaganda operations should cease. The White Operations were to carry on, being enough to deal with any remaining pockets of resistance. Atlantiksender and Soldatensender closed down on April 29th and 30th without any formal announcement.

Delmer held a party in the canteen at Milton Bryan; it was the first time that all the members from the various RUs had met. On 1 May he held a meeting of all the staff, telling them that the work they had done was to remain a secret, as it was feared that if the Germans found out too much they might claim the war had been won using propaganda, as they had done at the end of the First World War.

The staff at Milton Bryan then collected all the paperwork together and burnt it in the grounds of the compound. Because there was no official survey carried out we shall probably never know how effective the black operations were or whether they in fact helped shortened the war. However, with the considerable amount of information gathered from POW's it was clear that Atlantiksender and Soldatensender had a large audience and was in some instances more popular than Deutschlandsender, despite constant jamming by a rather worried Goebbels.

For a short period after the black operations had ceased the studios at Milton Bryan were used to send news to Germany via the DNB Hell-schreiber for insertion into the Allied controlled German press. At the end of the war the compound became home to former POW's, before they were repatriated - mainly U Boat officers and ratings, ironically the people that Atlantiksender had been aimed at. In 1949 it was used to billet Irish farm labourers and when they went the buildings were left to fall into ruin. In recent years the site has been taken over by the Scouts.

The buildings that housed the shortwave transmitters at Potsgrove still stand and are used for farm storage. The aerials have long gone. The Gawcott site was used as a government communications station up until recently, but this has now gone.

Aspidistra at Crowborough was used by the Diplomatic Wireless Service and the BBC to reinforce its European service until September 1982 when it was shut down, Harold Robin performing the switch-off ceremony. By 1986 the underground buildings had been stripped and have been refurbished by the Home Office possibly for storage of records.

Will the present or future owners of Dawn Edge, Larchfields, the Rookery and the other houses in and around Aspley Guise that had been requisitioned during the war, ever realise that their rooms once echoed to the voices of Germans, Italians, Romanians, and other foreign nationals as they wrote their scripts?

Will the customers at the Paris House Restaurant in the grounds of Woburn Abbey, a mere stone's throw from MB, know as they enjoy their meals that it was once home to a deserter of the Waffen SS, whose RU pretended to run a SW transmitter located behind the Eastern Front and operated by an anti-Hitler group of the Waffen SS?

I doubt it very much.

Bibliography

Black Boomerang. Sefton Delmer, 1962, Secker & Warburg.

The Black Game. Ellic Howe, 1982

Black Propaganda. Mark Kenyon. After the Battle, issue 75.

Imperial War Museum. Comprehensive collection of Black Propaganda material.

Photographs of Aspidistra, Diplomatic Wireless Service Museum, Bletchley Park.

Photographs of Milton Bryan Studios, Bletchley Park Archives.

Public Records Office, File FO898

Volksempfanger Wireless Sets. RAF Museum, Hendon.

Volksempfanger photographs, Bletchley Park Archives.

Volksischer Beobachter, forgery of, in Bletchley Park Archives

Woburn at War. Television documentary, Anglia TV 1987.

APPENDIX - RESEARCH UNITS

AUSTRIAN

A1.   RADIO ROTES WIEN. 2/10/41 TO 27/12/41. 62 PROGRAMMES.
      No further details available.

BELGIAN

B1.   RADIO VRIJSCHUTTER. 4/7/41 TO 8/6/44.
      BROADCAST 6 DAYS A WEEK.
      NUMBER OF PROGRAMMES UNKNOWN.
      The broadcasts were in Flemish. Its aim was to encourage resistance amongst the Flemish patriots. The station was very popular amongst the Flemish peasants and industrial workers. The transmissions were put out at 22.30 so as not to clash with the BBC and not to late for Flemish peasants 'bedtime'.

B2   SAMBRE ET MEUSE. 9/5/42 TO 4/6/44.
      TWO BROADCASTS DAILY, SIX DAYS A WEEK.
      The aim of this socialist RU was to stimulate resistance to the Germans within their country and avoid deportation to Germany. It also tried to keep the actions of the resistance movements within Belgium controlled and disciplined to prevent them from following the extreme communist movements.

BULGARIAN

X1.   VASIL LEVSKI. 6/11/41 TO 11/1/44. 762 PROGRAMMES.
      The main object of this left wing RU was to undermine the effectiveness of King Boris (until his death on 28/8/43) and the Bulgarian government. It also exposed their support of Germany. When King Boris died the station broadcast over a period of six days, the circumstances in which he died (allegedly) at the hands of the Germans. Although reports showed it was listened to in Bulgaria, the BBC was more popular. It was also believed the station was British.

X2.   THE VOICE OF NEW EUROPE. 2/7/43 TO 15/7/44.
      ONE 15 MINUTE NEWS BULLETIN BROADCAST DAILY.
      This RU gave the impression to the listener that it was a black German station broadcasting to Bulgaria. The station opened with the playing of the Bulgarian and German national anthems, followed by a series of news items including German High Command communique, some false, some doctored and others were genuine.

CZECH

RD. RADIO NAZDAR. 16/3/41 TO 28/9/41. 65 PROGRAMMES.
No further details available.

NOVA EUROPE (NO CODE No. OR LETTERS). 23/6/43 TO 30/6/44.
NUMBER OF PROGRAMMES UNKNOWN.
This RU operated as a pseudo-collaborator in such a way as to turn the Czechs against it . It purported to be broadcasting from inside the Protectorate.

DANISH

D1. RADIO DENMARK. 16/2/41 TO 27/4/42. 432 PROGRAMMES.
No further details available.

D2. DANISH FREEDOM. 1/7/42 TO 24/9/43. 291 PROGRAMMES.
The aim of this RU was to acquaint Danish listeners with the techniques in circulating news from the clandestine broadcasts. Although the evidence of reception was small, it did suggest the station was listened to and its contents discussed.

D3. RADIO SKAGERAK. 6/2/43 TO 5/5/43. 26 PROGRAMMES RECORDED.
No further details available.

D4. HJEMMEFRONTE RADIO. 6/12/42 TO 18/4/45.
No further details available.

DUTCH

H1. RADIO FLITSPUIT. 17/7/41 TO 18/8/42. 286 PROGRAMMES.
No further details available.

H2. FLUISTERGIDS. 6/2/43 TO 28/3/43. 30 PROGRAMMES RECORDED.
No further details available.

H3. BLAUWVOET. 24/3/43 TO 4/5/44.
NUMBER PROGRAMMES NOT AVAILABLE.
This RU gave the impression that it was run by a group of dissident collaborators who felt they had been let down by the Germans. It stirred up suspicion between collaborator groups and the Germans, and also between the rival groups of collaborators. It also encouraged desertion in the lower ranks of the collaborator parties in both Holland and Belgium, creating complications in the German administration.

FRENCH

F1. RADIO INCONNUE. 15/11/40 TO 10/1/44. 1145 PROGRAMMES.
Purported to be broadcasting from the Paris area. Programme content was subversive encouraging passive forms of resistance. It constantly attacked Marshal Petain and the Vichy regime. The existence of Radio Inconnue was never divulged to the Free French or General de Gaulle.

F2. RADIO TRAVAIL. 17/11/40 TO 21/5/42. 551 PROGRAMMES.
Purported to be located in the northern departments of occupied France. Its programme content reflected the revolutionary traditions of France, regularly attacking the Germans and like F1 encouraged passive forms of resistance and sabotage.

F3. LA FRANCE CATHOLIQUE. 1/7/41 TO 15/5/44. TWO BROADCASTS DAILY, NUMBER OF PROGRAMMES NOT AVAILABLE.
The speaker of this RU was a French priest, Father Lagrave. The aim of the station was to encourage resistance among the Catholics in France. In his talks there would be comparisons made between the methods of Hitler and Satan. Companies working for the Germans were advised to continue to operate normally thus providing employment for the French, but were asked to produce poor quality goods. German reports suggested the station was broadcast from the Vatican. Although aware of the stations existance the Vatican never denied these suggestions.

F4. RADIO GAULLE. 25/8/41 TO 15/11/42. 426 PROGRAMMES.
The speakers on this RU were members of the Free French Forces. The contents of the programmes were designed to train resistance groups.

F5. HONNEUR ET PATRIE. 11/10/42 TO 2/4/44. NUMBER OF PROGRAMMES UNKNOWN. TWO BROADCASTS DAILY.
Closely linked to the clandestine press in France, its purpose was to broadcast orders and directives of the Conseil de Resistance in London. Like F4 its aim was to instruct the French people in methods of underground warfare.

GERMAN

G1. DAS WAHRE DEUTSCHLAND. 26/5/40 TO 15/3/41. 294 PROGRAMMES.
Dr. Carl Spiecker's 'The True Germany' station. This was the first black radio station.

G2. SENDER DER EUROPAISCHEN REVOLUTION. 7/10/40 TO 22/6/42. 582 PROGRAMMES.
A left wing socialist station, its aim was to create passive resistance to the German war machine by encouraging factory workers to 'go slow'.

G3. GUSTAV SIEGFRIED EINS (GS1). 23/5/41 TO 18/11/43. 693 PROGRAMMES.
Delmer's first RU, the output of which was to create a growing split between the old conservatives within the army and the Nazi Party. The speaker called himself Der Chef and his language was very often coarse and obscene, exposing curruption high up in the Nazi Party.

G5. WEHRMACHTSENDER NORD. 9/5/42 TO 7/2/43. 275 PROGRAMMES.
This RU purported to be run by a German military unit stationed in Norway, its object was to broadcast news of home to the German soldiers stationed there. The idea was that it would paint a gloomy picture of what life was like back in Germany, thus lowering the morale of the listener.

G6. ASTROLOGIE UND OKKULTISMUS. 28/3/42 TO 19/4/42. 18 PROGRAMMES RECORDED BUT NEVER BROADCAST.
In the recordings a Margit Maas impersonated a spiritualist who had received messages from deceased members of the German armed forces for transmission to their bereaved families. She spoilt the recordings because she found it difficult to read the scripts without occasionally laughing.

G7. GERMAN PRIEST (CHRISTUS DER KONIG). 16/9/42 TO 28/4/45. NUMBER OF PROGRAMMES NOT AVAILABLE.
An Austrian Roman Catholic Priest, Father Andreas, wrote and broadcast the scripts. The broadcasts consisted of a short religious service followed by a brief talk in which listeners were told of the infamous things the which were being carried out by the Nazi Party:- The euthanasia program, the mating of unmarried girls in order to produce a Germanic master race etc. Unknown to Father Andreas Delmer had asked the SOE to instruct their rumour agents in neutral capitals the station was operated by the Vatican.

G8. WORKERS' STATION. 17/7/42 TO 23/3/43. 226 PROGRAMMES.
No further details available.

G9. KURZWELLENSENDER ATLANTIK (ATLANTIK SENDER). 22/3/43 TO 30/4/45. LINKED TO SOLDATENSENDER FROM 14/11/43.
Atlantik sender was aimed at the Kreigsmarine U Boat crews, unlike other German RU's it gave the impression to the listener it was a German forces radio station. It played popular music and regular news bulletins with subversive items inserted, in an effort to lower the morale of the listener. Soldatensender followed the same format but was chiefly for the German forces stationed in Europe to soften them up prior to the Allied invasion. All G9 programmes were broadcast live from Milton Bryan and Soldatensender Calais was transmitted on the medium wave band using the powerful Aspidistra transmitter at Crowborough.

G10. KAMPFGRUPPE YORCK WAFFEN SS. 11/12/43 TO 18/4/45. NUMBER OF PROGRAMMES NOT AVAILABLE AND TRANSMISSIONS ERRATIC.
This station was run by a Zech-Nenntwich, a former Waffen SS officer, who had deserted and smuggled into Sweden by the Poles. Although his story convinced the experts at the interrogation centres, he was received rather cautiously at Milton Bryan and kept away in near isolation at Paris House on the Woburn Estate. The station gave the impression that it was run by a small group of powerful Waffen SS officers who had turned against Hitler.

U1. HAGEDORN (HAWTHORN). 26/1/45 TO 27/4/45.
No further details available. Probably a pseudo-German resistance station.

HUNGARIAN

M1. MAGYAR NEMZET. 6/9/42 TO 7/1/45. 8 BROADCASTS ON SUNDAYS ONLY.
This RU was aimed at the middle classes of Hungary and claimed it was connected with the leading opposition newspaper of the same name, indirect advertisements for the station appearing in the paper. The object was to increase opposition to Germany and to reduce aid.

ITALIAN

W1. RADIO ITALIA. 16/11/40 TO 15/5/42. 545 PROGRAMMES.
This RU's main aim was to spread decremental stories about the Germans. It also encouraged listeners to buy and hoard items that were in short supply.

W2. RADIO LIBERTA. 8/6/41 TO 27/11/41. 168 PROGRAMMES.
This RU purported to be the mouthpiece of a group of young disillusioned Fascisti. Its main attack was on Mussolini, revealing intimate knowledge about his private life. As with W1 listeners were encouraged to hoard items that were in short supply. One item being radio valves! This advice was questionable because as an economic analyst pointed out, Italian industrial and agricultural workers owned less than 4% of the shortwave receivers in Italy.

W3. ANDREA VIAGHIELLO. 1/1/42 TO 14/3/43. 354 PROGRAMMES.
No further details available.

W4. ITALIA RISORGI. 6/2/43 TO 15/9/43. 152 PROGRAMMES.
The location of this station was purported to be in northern Italy and run by a group of anti-Fascists. Its object was to urge action against the Fascist regime. It also advocated the return to power of the House of Savoy. The station closed down a week before Italy unconditionally surrendered.

W4. cont'd RADIO LIVORNO (NO CODE NUMBER OR LETTER). 25/7/43 TO ? NUMBER OF PROGRAMMES UNKNOWN.

The aim of this RU was to give the impression the Germans were the real enemy and build up solidarity in the Italian navy. The station was under the direct control of the Naval Intelligence Division's 17z section. The station purported to be run by an Italian naval officer and a naval radio operator located in the Leghorn area. It is said it was this station that caused the Italian navy to surrender but this is speculation.

W5. GIUSTIZIA e LIBERTA. 27/7/43 TO 26/6/44. NUMBER OF PROGRAMMES UNKNOWN.

Purported to be run by a group of anti-Fascists belonging to the Giustizia e Liberta. It made out that it was in contact with all the active anti-Fascist organisations in Italy. It was run by 5 prominent members of the Giustizia e Liberta, their political knowledge and understanding of the situation in Italy was a great help to the PWE.

W6. INTRUDER INTO ITALIAN REPUBLICAN FASCIST RADIO. 18/9/43 TO 27/10/43. NUMBER OF PROGRAMMES NOT KNOWN.

A short lived RU, the first to use the powerful Aspidistra medium wave transmitter. It relayed the genuine NFR station and inserted subversive news items and talks. Items included an attack on the Vatican in the name of Fascism. It also broadcast false details about the Germans arranging the free distribution of food at Fascist headquarters in certain towns, the aim being to clog up roads used by the enemy for lines of communication. From the numerous come backs from monitors in Sweden, Switzerland, the USA and the BBC it was very successful, but because of the lack of trained operators the project had to be abandoned.

NORWEGIAN

N1. NORWEGIAN FREEDOM. 5/2/41 TO 16/12/42. 609 PROGRAMMES.

The object of the RU was to create opposition to the Germans in Norway. One successful reaction to the station was the '1918' campaign it ran in the autumn of 1942 in which it encouraged many Norwegians to daub walls with 1918, the year the Germans were defeated in the First World War. The station closed down when the exiled Norwegian government refused to allow the Norwegian staff to continue working unless it took control of the station.

POLISH

P1. ROZGLOSNIA POLSKA SWIT. 2/11/42 TO 25/11/44. NUMBER OF PROGRAMMES NOT AVAILABLE.

The cheif object of this RU was to pass information from London to the Polish underground movement. It also transmitted encoded messages from the exiled Polish government to the Directorate of Underground Warfare in Poland. The station was denounced by the Russians claiming it spoke for the aristocracy. The Russian policy in Poland, as with everywhere else, was to generate armed uprisings whatever the costs and P1 constantly issued warnings against this.

P2.   GLOS POLSKIEJ KOBIETY (THE VOICE OF POLISH WOMEN). 26/10/43 TO 30/5/44. NUMBER OF PROGRAMMES NOT KNOWN.
This RU was run by a group of Polish women, its main object was to feed information to the clandestine presses operating in Poland.

ROMAINIAN

R1.   FRATS ROMUN. 10/11/40 TO 20/7/43. 974 PROGRAMMES.
The output of this RU was openly anti-German, attacking them directly. R1 was taken over by R2.

R2.   PORUNCA MARESULULI (THE MARSHAL'S ORDER). 21/7/43 TO 26/6/44. NUMBER OF PROGRAMMES UNKNOWN.
The output of this RU was aimed at the middle and upper classes of Romania, it ran a number of successful rumour campaigns. For example, there was a protest from Budapest on the anti-Hungarian material that was broadcast by the RU in the name of Marshal Antonescu.

R3.   PRAHOVA. 18/10/43 TO 30/4/44. NUMBER OF PROGRAMMES NOT KNOWN.
The initial aim of this RU was to try and conserve the Romanian oil supplies by trying to reduce the supplies being sent to Germany. This was done by encouraging the workers to 'go slow' rather than use direct sabotage. The RU implied that it had the support of the Romanian government. Early in 1944 it introduced a policy advocating the use of violence and acts of direct sabotage not only on the oil supplies but also oil seed crops, cereals and the transport systems.

SLOVAK

S1.   BRADLO. 4/9/43 TO 19//7/44. NUMBER OF PROGRAMMES UNKNOWN.
The main object of this RU was to increase hatred of those who collaborated with the Germans. It also undermined the loyalty of Slovak troops serving with the Germany army and it encouraged the Slovak hatred of the Hungarians, adding to German difficulties.

YUGOSLAV

Y1. RADIO ZRINSKI. 31/5/41 TO 1/12/43. 906 PROGRAMMES.
The object of this RU was to undermine the Quisling government in Croatia. It had to close down because of the conflicting aims of Tito and Michailovitch.

Y2. RADIO SHUMADIA. 7/8/41 TO 19/11/43. 811 PROGRAMMES.
This RU was aimed at the middle classes of Belgrade. Its main object was to destroy the authority and prestige of the Nedic government and stall its attempt to generate Serb collaboration with the Germans. This RU was kept going by a single script writer/announcer due to the difficulty in finding suitable Serbs with the 'right outlook'. It also encouraged civil disobedience among provincial officials and exposed the bad working conditions at the German controlled Bor mines.

Y3. RADIO TRIGLAV. 23/8/41 TO 9/4/42. 211 PROGRAMMES
Nofurther details available.

Y4. YA STARO PRAVDO (FOR ANCIENT JUSTICE). 23/1/43 TO 19/12/43. ONE DAILY BROADCAST WITH TWO AT WEEKENDS.
The initial object of this RU was to undermine the morale of the Italians by spreading rumours using the Slovenes. After Italy surrendered the station tried to generate maximum collaboration between the Slovenes and the Italians against the Germans. During the Tunisian campaign the station made great efforts to compromise the Slovenes that were in the Italian army in the hope the Italian military authorities would withdraw the 20,000 Slovenes from front line duties and draft them into the Slovene labour camps in Italy. And in fact from June 1943 the Italian authorities did start sending new Slovene recruits to the labour camps.